Your name

This is what happened to me
when my parents got a divorce.

When I was little, I thought all families lived happily together forever.

My mom and dad stopped loving each other
when I was five years old.
They started to argue about everything.

I felt like it was all my fault.

Do you feel it is your fault your parents fight?

It hurt me to hear Mom and Dad angry.

Sometimes I felt like running away and never coming back.

Do you ever feel like running away? _____

One day, Mom said she was moving to the city and taking me with her.

I felt as if my heart was being torn in two.

It was very hard to say goodbye to my dad.

Please draw a picture of when your parents separated.

I thought Mom and Dad would go back together again if I were good.

I promised to pick up my toys and never cause trouble if Dad came back.

That didn't make any difference.

Then I began to feel angry.

It didn't seem fair that other kids had their Mom and Dad together in one home.

Do you often feel angry?   *At whom?*

_____   _____

I felt very lonely without Dad and my friends.

Mom brought home a puppy named "Ruffy"
to keep me company.

Who keeps you company when you are lonely?

_____

Mom started dating after the divorce.

I felt angry when her friends tried to tell me what to do.

I did not like anyone getting close to Mom.

I was hoping my parents would get back together if they didn't find anyone else.

Do you hope your parents will go back together?

After the divorce, Mom often yelled at me when she was tired or unhappy.

This gave me the stomach ache.
I would go hide in my bed.

Please draw a picture showing how you feel when Mom or Dad yells at you.

There was not much money after the divorce.
Mom found a job and I went to live with Dad.
I had to learn to take care of myself
and help around the house.

What are three things you do to help at home?

_____   _____   _____

I missed my mom a lot.

I wished for a helicopter so that I could fly back and forth between my parents.

How often do you think of your away parent?

Dad and I started spending more time together after the divorce.

I liked having Dad all to myself.

At first Dad and I spent a lot of time alone together. Then Dad fell in love with a lady named Joan who had a daughter, Nico.

Has your mom or dad found a new partner? _____

Nico and I felt left out after Dad and Joan married. We got into trouble at school and fought a lot at home.

Do you ever feel lonely or left out? _____

It was hard for me to share my home and my dad with another kid. I don't like anyone else coming in my bedroom unless I say so.

How would you feel about sharing your home with other kids?

We went to a family counselor who helped us understand and respect one another.

Who do you talk to about your feelings?

We agreed on some house rules to help us get along better. My life was more fun when we stopped fighting.

What are two rules in your home?

1. _____

2. _____

I asked Dad to spend more time alone with me. Now we play ball or go fishing every Saturday morning.

What do alone with your home parent?

My mom and dad are happier now than when they lived together.

I know that their divorce was not because of me. It would have happened anyway.

Are your parents happier now than before?

IT CAN WORK!

Divorce does hurt, but life is often much better afterwards.

It just takes time to work things out.

List two good things that have happened since your parents separated.

1. _____

2. _____

You and I are not alone. There are lots of us kids with divorced or separated parents.

What other kids do you know
whose parents are separated or divorced?

_____

_____

_____

This might be a good time to talk
with someone about your own feelings.

Phone toll free 1-800-682-0029 for additional information or to place an order.
Full return privileges on all titles. 300,000 IN PRINT, USED BY 5,000 SCHOOLS.

SPECIAL PACKAGE OFFERS

Counselor's 7 Pack • Activity Books #1 to #7	$39.15
Divorce Support 4 Pack • Activity Books #2 to #5	$22.60
Library 32 Pack • 4 of Activity Books #1 to #8	$175.00
AIDS Classroom Kit • (Photocopy Permit)	$344.95

50 Activity Book #8 • 1 Teaching Guide • 1 Photocopy Master
1 Life Before Death Workbook

This kit was developed for group presentations where low cost consumable materials are important.
The purchase of this kit carries the right to reproduce the Uncle Jerry Has AIDS book.
The license to photocopy is specific to the purchaser of one location (i.e. one *school* — not *district*).

ACTIVITY BOOKS FOR CHILDREN IN DISTRESS
Grade Appropriate K-6

TITLE	QUANTITY	PRICE	TOTAL
1. **Saying Goodbye** (Bereavement)	_____	$5.95	_____
2. **Let's Talk** (Early Divorce)	_____	$5.95	_____
3. **My Story** (Divorce & Remarriage)	_____	$5.95	_____
4. **Alone Together** (Single Parent)	_____	$5.95	_____
5. **All Together** (Blended Family)	_____	$5.95	_____
6. **Feeling Good** (Self Esteem)	_____	$5.95	_____
7. **My Secret** (Parent Drug Abuse)	_____	$5.95	_____
8. **Uncle Jerry Has AIDS** (Emotion)	_____	$5.95	_____

SUPPORTIVE REFERENCES FOR ADULTS

TITLE	QUANTITY	PRICE	TOTAL
Death & Dying 4 Pack #1, #9, #10 & #11	_____	$38.95	_____
9. **Life & Death** (300 Quotes)	_____	$13.95	_____
10. **Life Before Death Workbook**	_____	$13.95	_____
11. **Caregiver's Handbook**	_____	$6.95	_____

TOTAL CHARGES _____
Shipping Charge - Refer to Catalogue _____
G.S.T. 7% _____
TOTAL BILLING _____

FULL REMITTANCE MUST ACCOMPANY ORDERS FOR $30.00 OR LESS

SPECIAL INSTRUCTIONS: Purchase Order No., Shipping Instructions

_____

Name _____ Phone _____ Fax _____

Organization _____

Street _____

City _____ Province _____ Postal Code _____

MARVIN MELNYK ASSOCIATES LTD.
P.O. Box 220, Queenston, ON L0S 1L0 • Phone: 1-416-262-4964 • Fax: 1-416-262-5303